Wedding Planner
Checklist

THIS PLANNER BELONGS TO

Wedding Date

_____ / _____

Time:

_____

Wedding Venue

_____

Wedding Contact

● **Wedding Planner**

Name: ....   Phone: ....

Email: ....   Location: ....

Web: ....

● **Reception Venue**

Name: ....   Phone: ....

Email: ....   Location: ....

Web: ....

● **Caterer**

Name: ....   Phone: ....

Email: ....   Location: ....

Web: ....

● **Ceremony Venue**

Name: ....   Phone: ....

Email: ....   Location: ....

Web: ....

● **Officiant**

Name: ....   Phone: ....

Email: ....   Location: ....

Web: ....

● **Photographer**

Name: ....   Phone: ....

Email: ....   Location: ....

Web: ....

● **Videographer**

Name: ....   Phone: ....

Email: ....   Location: ....

Web: ....

● **Florist**

Name: ....   Phone: ....

Email: ....   Location: ....

Web: ....

Wedding Contact

● Shop / Dress Designer

Name: ....   Phone: ....

Email: ....   Location: ....

Web: ....

● Bridal Attier

Name: ....   Phone: ....

Email: ....   Location: ....

Web: ....

● Bridal Jewelry

Name: ....   Phone: ....

Email: ....   Location: ....

Web: ....

● Hair Stylist

Name: ....   Phone: ....

Email: ....   Location: ....

Web: ....

● Makeup Artist

Name: ....   Phone: ....

Email: ....   Location: ....

Web: ....

● Stationary Designer

Name: ....   Phone: ....

Email: ....   Location: ....

Web: ....

● DJ Party Entertainment

Name: ....   Phone: ....

Email: ....   Location: ....

Web: ....

● Honeymoon- Hotel/Resort

Name: ....   Phone: ....

Email: ....   Location: ....

Web: ....

Wedding Contact

● **Welcome Party Venue**

Name: ....   Phone: ....

Email: ....   Location: ....

Web: ....

● **Rehearsal Dinner Venue:**

Name: ....   Phone: ....

Email: ....   Location: ....

Web: ....

● **Wedding cake:**

Name: ....   Phone: ....

Email: ....   Location: ....

Web: ....

● **Other:**

Name: ....   Phone: ....

Email: ....   Location: ....

Web: ....

●

Name: ....   Phone: ....

Email: ....   Location: ....

Web: ....

●

Name: ....   Phone: ....

Email: ....   Location: ....

Web: ....

●

Name: ....   Phone: ....

Email: ....   Location: ....

Web: ....

●

Name: ....   Phone: ....

Email: ....   Location: ....

Web: ....

Important Date

Date:

Date:

Date:

Note

_____

_____

_____

_____

Date:

Date:

Date:

_____

_____

_____

_____

_____

_____

Date:

Date:

Date:

_____

_____

_____

_____

_____

Date:

Date:

Date:

_____

_____

_____

_____

_____

_____

Date:

Date:

Date:

_____

_____

_____

_____

Important Date

Note

Date:

Date:

Date:

Date:

Date:

Date:

Date:

Date:

Date:

Date:

Date:

Date:

Date:

Date:

Date:

 # Wedding Budget

Details	Cost	Deposit	Remainder

Note & Special Reminder:

Wedding Budget

Details	Cost	Deposit	Remainder

Note & Special Reminder: ....
....
....
....
....

 # Wedding Budget

Details	Cost	Deposit	Remainder

Note & Special Reminder:
....
....
....
....
....

Wedding Budget

Details	Cost	Deposit	Remainder

Note & Special Reminder: ....
....
....
....
....

 # Wedding Budget

Details	Cost	Deposit	Remainder

Note & Special Reminder: ....
....
....
....
....

Wedding Budget

Details	Cost	Deposit	Remainder

Note & Special Reminder: ....
....
....
....
....
....

 # Wedding Budget

Details	Cost	Deposit	Remainder

Note & Special Reminder:
....
....
....
....
....
....

Wedding Budget

Details	Cost	Deposit	Remainder

Note & Special Reminder: ....
....
....
....
....
....

 # Wedding Budget

Details	Cost	Deposit	Remainder

Note & Special Reminder: ....
....
....
....
....
....

Wedding Budget

Details	Cost	Deposit	Remainder

Note & Special Reminder: ....
....
....
....
....

Expense Snapshot
Ceremony Expense Tracker

Details	Budget	Cost	Deposit	Balance	Due Date
Officiant Gratuity					
Marriage License					
Venue Cost					
Flowers					
Decorations					

Note & Special Reminder:

Expense Snapshot
Reception Expense Tracker

Details	Budget	Cost	Deposit	Balance	Due Date
Venue Fee					
Catering					
Bar / Beverages					
Cake / Cutting Fee					
Decorations					
Rental					
Bartender Stuff					

Note & Special Reminder: ....
....
....
....
....
....

Checklist
12 Month Before

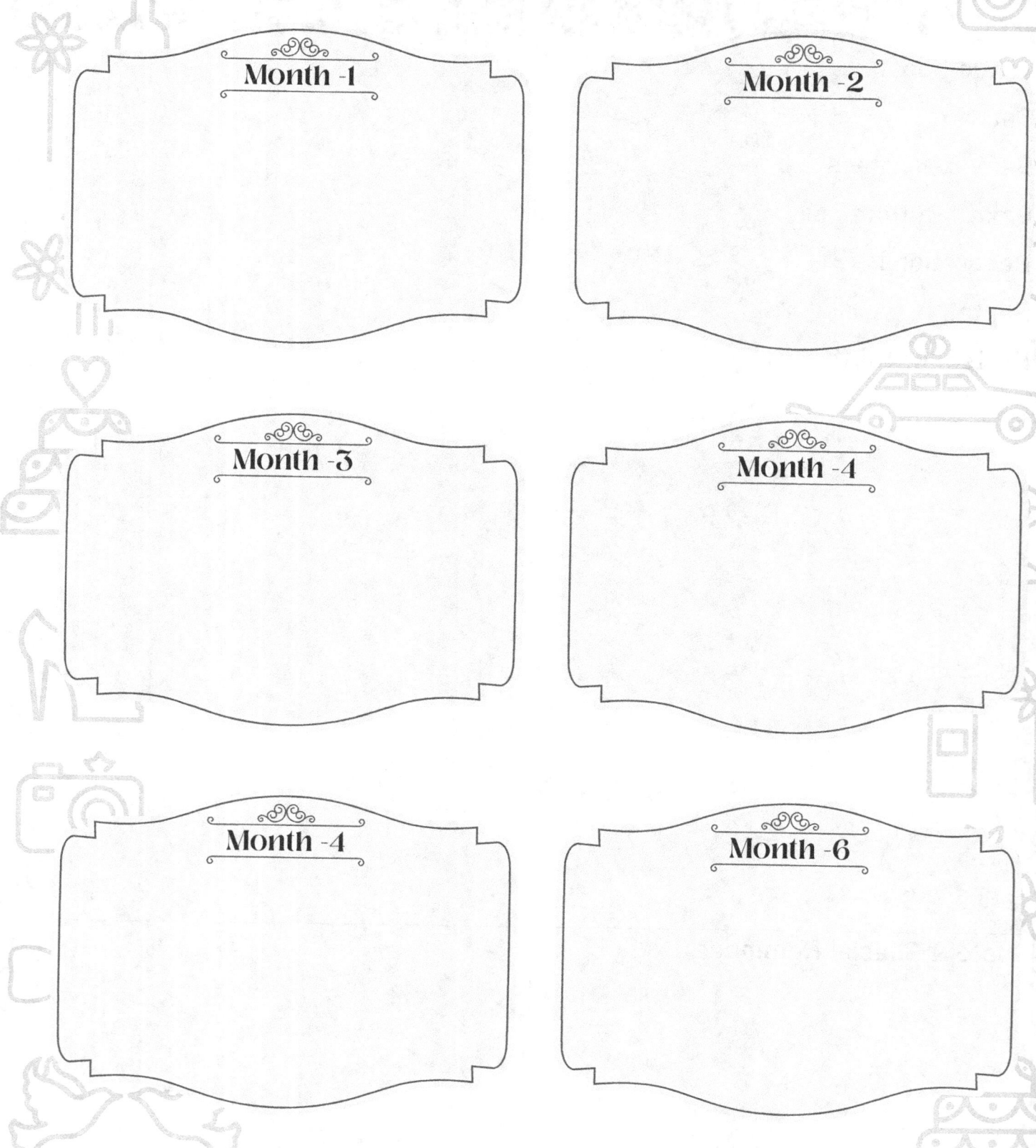

Month -1

Month -2

Month -3

Month -4

Month -4

Month -6

Checklist
12 Month Before

Month -7

Month -8

Month -9

Month -10

Month -11

Month -12

Guest List

Name	Phone	Email/Address

Guest List

Name	Phone	Email/Address

 # Guest List

Name	Phone	Email/Address
....	....	....
....	....	....
....	....	....
....	....	....
....	....	....
....	....	....
....	....	....
....	....	....
....	....	....
....	....	....
....	....	....
....	....	....
....	....	....
....	....	....
....	....	....
....	....	....
....	....	....
....	....	....

Guest List

Name	Phone	Email/Address

 # Guest List

Name	Phone	Email/Address

 # Guest List

Name	Phone	Email/Address
....	....	....
....	....	....
....	....	....
....	....	....
....	....	....
....	....	....
....	....	....
....	....	....
....	....	....
....	....	....
....	....	....
....	....	....
....	....	....
....	....	....
....	....	....
....	....	....
....	....	....
....	....	....
....	....	....

 # Guest List

Name	Phone	Email/Address

Guest List

Name	Phone	Email/Address

 # Guest List

Name	Phone	Email/Address

 # Guest List

Name	Phone	Email/Address

 # Guest List

Name	Phone	Email/Address

Guest List

Name	Phone	Email/Address

To Do List

Planning Notes

To Do List

Planning Notes

To Do List

- ♡ --
- ♡ --
- ♡ --
- ♡ --
- ♡ --
- ♡ --
- ♡ --
- ♡ --
- ♡ --
- ♡ --
- ♡ --
- ♡ --
- ♡ --
- ♡ --
- ♡ --

- ♡ --
- ♡ --
- ♡ --
- ♡ --
- ♡ --
- ♡ --
- ♡ --
- ♡ --
- ♡ --
- ♡ --
- ♡ --
- ♡ --
- ♡ --
- ♡ --
- ♡ --

Planning Notes

To Do List

Planning Notes

To Do List

- ♡ --
- ♡ --
- ♡ --
- ♡ --
- ♡ --
- ♡ --
- ♡ --
- ♡ --
- ♡ --
- ♡ --
- ♡ --
- ♡ --
- ♡ --
- ♡ --
- ♡ --

- ♡ --
- ♡ --
- ♡ --
- ♡ --
- ♡ --
- ♡ --
- ♡ --
- ♡ --
- ♡ --
- ♡ --
- ♡ --
- ♡ --
- ♡ --
- ♡ --
- ♡ --

Planning Notes

To Do List

Planning Notes

To Do List

- ♡ _____
- ♡ _____
- ♡ _____
- ♡ _____
- ♡ _____
- ♡ _____
- ♡ _____
- ♡ _____
- ♡ _____
- ♡ _____
- ♡ _____
- ♡ _____
- ♡ _____
- ♡ _____
- ♡ _____
- ♡ _____

- ♡ _____
- ♡ _____
- ♡ _____
- ♡ _____
- ♡ _____
- ♡ _____
- ♡ _____
- ♡ _____
- ♡ _____
- ♡ _____
- ♡ _____
- ♡ _____
- ♡ _____
- ♡ _____
- ♡ _____
- ♡ _____

Planning Notes

To Do List

- ♡ ....
- ♡ ....
- ♡ ....
- ♡ ....
- ♡ ....
- ♡ ....
- ♡ ....
- ♡ ....
- ♡ ....
- ♡ ....
- ♡ ....
- ♡ ....
- ♡ ....
- ♡ ....
- ♡ ....
- ♡ ....
- ♡ ....

- ♡ ....
- ♡ ....
- ♡ ....
- ♡ ....
- ♡ ....
- ♡ ....
- ♡ ....
- ♡ ....
- ♡ ....
- ♡ ....
- ♡ ....
- ♡ ....
- ♡ ....
- ♡ ....
- ♡ ....
- ♡ ....
- ♡ ....

Planning Notes

To Do List

Planning Notes

To Do List

♡ ------------------------------------
♡ ------------------------------------
♡ ------------------------------------
♡ ------------------------------------
♡ ------------------------------------
♡ ------------------------------------
♡ ------------------------------------
♡ ------------------------------------
♡ ------------------------------------
♡ ------------------------------------
♡ ------------------------------------
♡ ------------------------------------
♡ ------------------------------------
♡ ------------------------------------
♡ ------------------------------------
♡ ------------------------------------

♡ ------------------------------------
♡ ------------------------------------
♡ ------------------------------------
♡ ------------------------------------
♡ ------------------------------------
♡ ------------------------------------
♡ ------------------------------------
♡ ------------------------------------
♡ ------------------------------------
♡ ------------------------------------
♡ ------------------------------------
♡ ------------------------------------
♡ ------------------------------------
♡ ------------------------------------
♡ ------------------------------------
♡ ------------------------------------

Planning Notes

To Do List

- ♡ ....
- ♡ ....
- ♡ ....
- ♡ ....
- ♡ ....
- ♡ ....
- ♡ ....
- ♡ ....
- ♡ ....
- ♡ ....
- ♡ ....
- ♡ ....
- ♡ ....
- ♡ ....
- ♡ ....
- ♡ ....

- ♡ ....
- ♡ ....
- ♡ ....
- ♡ ....
- ♡ ....
- ♡ ....
- ♡ ....
- ♡ ....
- ♡ ....
- ♡ ....
- ♡ ....
- ♡ ....
- ♡ ....
- ♡ ....
- ♡ ....
- ♡ ....

Planning Notes

To Do List

- ♥ --
- ♥ --
- ♥ --
- ♥ --
- ♥ --
- ♥ --
- ♥ --
- ♥ --
- ♥ --
- ♥ --
- ♥ --
- ♥ --
- ♥ --
- ♥ --
- ♥ --
- ♥ --
- ♥ --

- ♥ --
- ♥ --
- ♥ --
- ♥ --
- ♥ --
- ♥ --
- ♥ --
- ♥ --
- ♥ --
- ♥ --
- ♥ --
- ♥ --
- ♥ --
- ♥ --
- ♥ --
- ♥ --
- ♥ --

Planning Notes

To Do List

- ♡ --
- ♡ --
- ♡ --
- ♡ --
- ♡ --
- ♡ --
- ♡ --
- ♡ --
- ♡ --
- ♡ --
- ♡ --
- ♡ --
- ♡ --
- ♡ --
- ♡ --
- ♡ --
- ♡ --

- ♡ --
- ♡ --
- ♡ --
- ♡ --
- ♡ --
- ♡ --
- ♡ --
- ♡ --
- ♡ --
- ♡ --
- ♡ --
- ♡ --
- ♡ --
- ♡ --
- ♡ --
- ♡ --
- ♡ --

Planning Notes

To Do List

Planning Notes

To Do List

Planning Notes

To Do List

- ♡ ....
- ♡ ....
- ♡ ....
- ♡ ....
- ♡ ....
- ♡ ....
- ♡ ....
- ♡ ....
- ♡ ....
- ♡ ....
- ♡ ....
- ♡ ....
- ♡ ....
- ♡ ....
- ♡ ....
- ♡ ....

- ♡ ....
- ♡ ....
- ♡ ....
- ♡ ....
- ♡ ....
- ♡ ....
- ♡ ....
- ♡ ....
- ♡ ....
- ♡ ....
- ♡ ....
- ♡ ....
- ♡ ....
- ♡ ....
- ♡ ....
- ♡ ....

Planning Notes

To Do List

Planning Notes

To Do List

- ....
- ....
- ....
- ....
- ....
- ....
- ....
- ....
- ....
- ....
- ....
- ....
- ....
- ....
- ....
- ....

- ....
- ....
- ....
- ....
- ....
- ....
- ....
- ....
- ....
- ....
- ....
- ....
- ....
- ....
- ....
- ....

Planning Notes

To Do List

- _____
- _____
- _____
- _____
- _____
- _____
- _____
- _____
- _____
- _____
- _____
- _____
- _____
- _____
- _____
- _____

- _____
- _____
- _____
- _____
- _____
- _____
- _____
- _____
- _____
- _____
- _____
- _____
- _____
- _____
- _____
- _____

Planning Notes

To Do List

Planning Notes

To Do List

♡ --

♡ --

♡ --

♡ --

♡ --

♡ --

♡ --

♡ --

♡ --

♡ --

♡ --

♡ --

♡ --

♡ --

♡ --

♡ --

♡ --

♡ --

♡ --

♡ --

♡ --

♡ --

♡ --

♡ --

♡ --

♡ --

♡ --

♡ --

♡ --

♡ --

♡ --

♡ --

Planning Notes

To Do List

- ♡ ....
- ♡ ....
- ♡ ....
- ♡ ....
- ♡ ....
- ♡ ....
- ♡ ....
- ♡ ....
- ♡ ....
- ♡ ....
- ♡ ....
- ♡ ....
- ♡ ....
- ♡ ....
- ♡ ....
- ♡ ....

- ♡ ....
- ♡ ....
- ♡ ....
- ♡ ....
- ♡ ....
- ♡ ....
- ♡ ....
- ♡ ....
- ♡ ....
- ♡ ....
- ♡ ....
- ♡ ....
- ♡ ....
- ♡ ....
- ♡ ....
- ♡ ....

Planning Notes

To Do List

- ....
- ....
- ....
- ....
- ....
- ....
- ....
- ....
- ....
- ....
- ....
- ....
- ....
- ....
- ....
- ....
- ....

- ....
- ....
- ....
- ....
- ....
- ....
- ....
- ....
- ....
- ....
- ....
- ....
- ....
- ....
- ....
- ....
- ....

Planning Notes

To Do List

- ♡ ------------------------------------
- ♡ ------------------------------------
- ♡ ------------------------------------
- ♡ ------------------------------------
- ♡ ------------------------------------
- ♡ ------------------------------------
- ♡ ------------------------------------
- ♡ ------------------------------------
- ♡ ------------------------------------
- ♡ ------------------------------------
- ♡ ------------------------------------
- ♡ ------------------------------------
- ♡ ------------------------------------
- ♡ ------------------------------------
- ♡ ------------------------------------
- ♡ ------------------------------------
- ♡ ------------------------------------

- ♡ ------------------------------------
- ♡ ------------------------------------
- ♡ ------------------------------------
- ♡ ------------------------------------
- ♡ ------------------------------------
- ♡ ------------------------------------
- ♡ ------------------------------------
- ♡ ------------------------------------
- ♡ ------------------------------------
- ♡ ------------------------------------
- ♡ ------------------------------------
- ♡ ------------------------------------
- ♡ ------------------------------------
- ♡ ------------------------------------
- ♡ ------------------------------------
- ♡ ------------------------------------
- ♡ ------------------------------------

Planning Notes

To Do List

- [ ] ---------------------------------
- [ ] ---------------------------------
- [ ] ---------------------------------
- [ ] ---------------------------------
- [ ] ---------------------------------
- [ ] ---------------------------------
- [ ] ---------------------------------
- [ ] ---------------------------------
- [ ] ---------------------------------
- [ ] ---------------------------------
- [ ] ---------------------------------
- [ ] ---------------------------------
- [ ] ---------------------------------
- [ ] ---------------------------------
- [ ] ---------------------------------
- [ ] ---------------------------------
- [ ] ---------------------------------

Planning Notes

To Do List

♡ --
♡ --
♡ --
♡ --
♡ --
♡ --
♡ --
♡ --
♡ --
♡ --
♡ --
♡ --
♡ --
♡ --
♡ --

♡ --
♡ --
♡ --
♡ --
♡ --
♡ --
♡ --
♡ --
♡ --
♡ --
♡ --
♡ --
♡ --
♡ --
♡ --

Planning Notes

To Do List

Planning Notes

To Do List

Gift List

Date	Gift Description	Given by	Thank You Sent
			♡
			♡
			♡
			♡
			♡
			♡
			♡
			♡
			♡
			♡
			♡
			♡
			♡
			♡
			♡
			♡
			♡

Note & Special Reminder: ....
....
....
....
....
....

Gift List

Date	Gift Description	Given by	Thank You Sent
			♡
			♡
			♡
			♡
			♡
			♡
			♡
			♡
			♡
			♡
			♡
			♡
			♡
			♡
			♡
			♡
			♡
			♡

Note & Special Reminder: ....
....
....
....
....
....

Gift List

Date	Gift Description	Given by	Thank You Sent
			♡
			♡
			♡
			♡
			♡
			♡
			♡
			♡
			♡
			♡
			♡
			♡
			♡
			♡
			♡
			♡
			♡

Note & Special Reminder:

Gift List

Date	Gift Description	Given by	Thank You Sent
			♡
			♡
			♡
			♡
			♡
			♡
			♡
			♡
			♡
			♡
			♡
			♡
			♡
			♡
			♡
			♡
			♡

Note & Special Reminder: ....
....
....
....
....
....

Gift List

Date	Gift Description	Given by	Thank You Sent
			♡
			♡
			♡
			♡
			♡
			♡
			♡
			♡
			♡
			♡
			♡
			♡
			♡
			♡
			♡
			♡
			♡

Note & Special Reminder: ....
....
....
....
....

Gift List

Date	Gift Description	Given by	Thank You Sent
			♡
			♡
			♡
			♡
			♡
			♡
			♡
			♡
			♡
			♡
			♡
			♡
			♡
			♡
			♡
			♡
			♡

Note & Special Reminder: ....
....
....
....
....
....

 # Gift List

Date	Gift Description	Given by	Thank You Sent
			♡
			♡
			♡
			♡
			♡
			♡
			♡
			♡
			♡
			♡
			♡
			♡
			♡
			♡
			♡
			♡
			♡

Note & Special Reminder: ....
....
....
....
....

Gift List

Date	Gift Description	Given by	Thank You Sent
			♡
			♡
			♡
			♡
			♡
			♡
			♡
			♡
			♡
			♡
			♡
			♡
			♡
			♡
			♡
			♡
			♡

Note & Special Reminder: ....
....
....
....
....
....

Gift List

Date	Gift Description	Given by	Thank You Sent
			♡
			♡
			♡
			♡
			♡
			♡
			♡
			♡
			♡
			♡
			♡
			♡
			♡
			♡
			♡
			♡
			♡
			♡

Note & Special Reminder: ....
....
....
....
....
....

 # Gift List

Date	Gift Description	Given by	Thank You Sent
			♡
			♡
			♡
			♡
			♡
			♡
			♡
			♡
			♡
			♡
			♡
			♡
			♡
			♡
			♡
			♡
			♡
			♡

Note & Special Reminder:
....
....
....
....
....

 # Gift List

Date	Gift Description	Given by	Thank You Sent
			♡
			♡
			♡
			♡
			♡
			♡
			♡
			♡
			♡
			♡
			♡
			♡
			♡
			♡
			♡
			♡
			♡

Note & Special Reminder: ....
....
....
....
....

Thank you!

We hope you enjoyed our book.

As a small family company, your feedback is very important to us .

Please let us know how you like our book at :

pickme.readme@gmail.com

"A successful marriage
is an edifice that must be
rebuilt every day"

- Andre Maurois-